Table of Contents

Introduction

As you can tell from the title, this cookbook is targeted towards all those people who want to enjoy some Instant Pot recipes for a healthier lifestyle. In today's ever-changing society, everyone is so busy that they find it hard to prepare a meal that not only satisfies their craving but also benefits their physical and mental condition. Most of us lack the time to prepare a fine home-cooked meal, so we indulge ourselves in bad eating habits and choices, like fast food, frozen meals, or junk food items.

All these unhealthy choices are a major cause of declining health and obesity in general. So, for many busy people, the major hurdle is to cook food in a shorter time period that is healthy. Well, if you are facing these all issues, then this book is a gateway to success.

As we are introducing a very fast and healthy way of preparing meals at home, that does not require much time, and guess what, it offers hands-free cooking.

With the basic aim of providing some fast and easy home-cooked meals, we have introduced over 70 recipes in this cookbook to make your experience with your Instant Pot a great one. But, before jumping into the cooking process, it is very crucial to know what the instant Pot does and how to operate it properly.

The first question most people raise is this: what is an Instant Pot? It is a single appliance with multiple purposes. It can perform the functions of seven cooking appliances. It is a steamer, pressure cooker, rice cooker, and even a warming pot. It speeds up cooking time tenfold and uses less than 70-80 percent of energy usually required.

You can find a lot of manufacturers in the market that produce different pressure cookers, not just the Instant Pot. In general, pressure cookers are very smart, time-effective, and budget-friendly appliances used by billions of people around the world. If you are a busy person or want to prepare a quick meal, then it is the right choice for you. It definitely saves a lot of time. Listed below are some potential benefits of using this appliance as a cooking tool.

Instant Pot Benefits

1. It reduces the overall time of cooking.
2. It is an energy-efficient appliance.
3. It preserves the nutrients in the food with great flavor and texture.
4. It is a very quick and clean process of cooking food.
5. You will have a hands-free and pleasant experience while cooking your meal.
6. It is easy to wash.
7. It's a very simple appliance with easy button functions.

What the Buttons Mean

After knowing about some potential benefits, you might be thinking about giving the Instant Pot a try, but before that, you need to get to know the buttons and how they work.

(+) and the **(–)** buttons are used to set and change the cooking time.

"ADJUST" button is used to change the temperature.

"PRESSURE" button is used to change the pressure from low to high.

"MANUAL" button adjusts the setting related to cooking from low to high using **"PRESSURE"** button.

"SAUTEE" button is used to sauté the ingredients. The machine automatically adjusts itself to normal. Therefore, you need to use a **"SAUTEE"** button to change the heat.

"SLOW COOK" button is used for slow cooking.

"STEAM" button is used to steam food.

Every meal has its own heat and time requirements which you can adjust using the **ADJUST** and **PRESSURE** buttons.

Steam Releasing Options

There are two options available here. One is **Quick Release**, and another is **Natural Release**. In the natural release method, the timer beeps, and you wait a few minutes, letting the steam escape without doing anything. It takes almost 10 minutes for the steam to release naturally.

With quick release you release the pot handle by turning it from sealing to vent. It only takes a minute for the steam to be released using this method.

Instant Pot Maintenance

The maintenance of any appliance is very crucial for its long-lasting and effective performance.

Here are some maintenance tips for your instant pot.

- Unplug the Instant Pot before cleaning it.
- Always hand-wash the appliance and use warm water and soap for fine cleaning.
- Always remove the steam release handle before washing.
- To remove bad smells or odors from a pressure cooker, wash it with a mixture of baking soda and water.

Instant Pot Do's and Don'ts

- While using the Instant Pot, never leave the house unattended.
- Don't pressure-fry food in the pot.
- Don't fill your instant Pot beyond the maximum capacity. Always leave a good amount of space, as food expands while cooking. The maximum capacity line is usually printed on the Instant Pot.
- Regularly put some water in an Instant Pot to maintain its pressure.
- Use a clean Instant Pot when cooking every meal.
- Replace the sealing ring every 15 months.
- Always insert the sealing ring before cooking any meal.
- The instant Pot anti-block shield should be properly mounted on a steam release pipe.

Instant Pot Terminology for Beginners

If you are a new user of this appliance, then you should know the following Instant Pot terminology:

IP stands for the Instant Pot.

QR is known as a quick release.

NR or **NPR** is known as a natural release (natural pressure release). **10-minute NPR** is referred to releasing the pressure on its own in 10 minutes.

HP is called high pressure.

The Trivet is the rack that users place inside the Instant Pot.

The Seal is sealing ring for the Instant Pot lid.

The Pin is the float valve.

EPC is stands for electric pressure cooker

Handle or vent is a handle on the lid. You turn it to seal the pot.

The Shield is the metal that covers the steam release valve.

PIP is used when food is placed in the bowl before putting into the instant pot.

The Sling is terminology for an aluminum foil strip.

PC stands for pressure cooker

Nut bag is a mesh bag used while making yogurt.

A Pothead is an Instant Pot user.

Instant Pot Options

Which pressure cooker is best for daily use is the most important question that needs to be answered. There are numerous options available in the market and online, where companies strive to provide the best quality pressure cooker at very reasonable prices. With all these options in mind, it's best to keep the overall size and function in mind. Below is a model chart of different pressure cookers along with their features to help you to decide which the best fit for your home.

Options	ULTRA 10-In-1	DUO Plus 9-In-1	SMART Million-In-1	DUO 7-In-1	LUX 6-In1
Variable Temperature	●		●		
Sterilizer	●	●			
Makes Yogurt	●	●	●	●	
Cook Food at Low Pressure	●	●	●	●	

Options	ULTRA 10-In-1	DUO Plus 9-In-1	SMART Million-In-1	DUO 7-In-1	LUX 6-In1
Cook Food at High Pressure	•	•	•	•	•
Sauté Button	•	•	•	•	•
Keeps Warm	•	•	•	•	•
Slow Cook	•	•	•	•	•
Steam	•	•	•	•	•
Rice Maker	•	•	•	•	•
Stainless Steel	•	•	•	•	•
Lid Rest in Handle	•	•	•	•	
Self-Closing Valve	•				

Where to Buy an Instant Pot?

No doubt an Instant Pot or any other pressure cooker is a magical device that makes you fall in love with it. Many Instant Pots and other pressure cookers are sold online on Amazon. Currently, two Instant Pot models are in the top 10 bestselling Kitchen items on Amazon. Local retail stores are also a very good option to buy an Instant Pot.

Instant Pot Pressure Cooking Time list

ITEMS	TIME
Red Meat	25-40 minutes
White meat	10-15 minutes
Fish	3 Minutes
Egg	2-4 minutes
Pasta /Noodles	5 minutes
Pork	55 minutes
Brown rice	25 minutes
Grains /lentils	10-30 minutes
Rice	15 minutes

The Dirty Dozen and Clean Fifteen

The Environmental Working Group's Shopper's Guide to Pesticides in Produce™ is a very smart guide that lists and ranks 48 fruits and vegetables according to the grade of toxic pesticide contamination. The guide is determined by tests done on more than 35,200 fruit and vegetable samples by the U.S. Department of Agriculture and Food and Drug Administration. Tests for pesticides are done on produce samples when they are thoroughly washed, peeled, packaged, and ready to be eaten. Pesticide residues can still be detected on ready-to-be-sold fruits and veggies. The EWG's Shopper's Guide helps buyers make the best choices when buying produce, helping them reduce their family's exposure to toxic pesticides.

Since EWG's start in 1993, they have constantly fought for consumer's rights to eat healthier fruits and vegetables. The EWG updates their list every year, their first report coming out in 1993. The report, Pesticides in Children's Foods, played an important role in Congress setting up the Food Quality Protection Act two years later. This law gave regulatory authority to the Environmental Protection Agency to ensure that pesticides used in foods aren't harmful to babies and children. The EWG's research found weed killers in Midwestern tap water and carcinogenic pesticides in food for babies. Even though EWG is proud to have played a role in this monumental step towards healthier produce, their work is far from done. Farmers still use huge amounts of toxic pesticides on fruits and vegetables that are being detected by the USDA. It's because of this reason that EWG updates their Shopper's Guide each year. It's self-explanatory why this guide has received a lot of media attention. The EWG makes it their purpose to investigate pesticides and other harmful chemicals that can damage health that could otherwise be unknown to the population.

Dirty Dozen and Clean Fifteen

Here is a short list of fruits and vegetables you can buy in non-organic form, this produces have a protective outer layer that is used as a defense against pesticides.

EWG's 2017 Shopper's Guide to Pesticides in Produce™

Clean Fifteen		Dirty Dozen	
1	Sweet Corn*	1	Strawberries
2	Avocados	2	Spinach
3	Pineapples	3	Nectarines
4	Cabbage	4	Apples
5	Onions	5	Peaches
6	Sweet peas frozen	6	Pears
7	Papayas*	7	Cherries
8	Asparagus	8	Grapes
9	Mangos	9	Celery
10	Eggplant	10	Tomatoes
11	Honeydew Melon	11	Sweet bell peppers
12	Kiwi	12	Potatoes
13	Cantaloupe		Hot Peppers +
14	Cauliflower		
15	Grapefruit		

* A small amount of sweet corn, papaya and summer squash sold in the United States is produced from genetically modified seeds. If you want to avoid genetically modified produce buy organic varieties of these crops.

Cooking Measurement Conversion (Approximate)

Measurement

CUP	OUNCES	MILLILITERS	TABLESPOONS	TEASPOONS
1/16 cup	1/2 oz	15 ml	1	3
1/8 cup	1 oz	30 ml	3	9
1/4 cup	2 oz	59 ml	4	12
1/3 cup	2.5 oz	79 ml	5.5	5 Tbls + 1 tsp
3/8 cup	3 oz	90 ml	6	18
1/2 cup	4 oz	118 ml	8	24
2/3 cup	5 oz	158 ml	11	10 Tbls+2 tsp
3/4 cup	6 oz	177 ml	12	36
1 cup	8 oz	240 ml	16	48
2 cup	16 oz	480 ml	32	96
4 cup	32 oz	960 ml	64	192
5 cup	40 oz	1180 ml	80	240
6 cup	48 oz	1420 ml	96	288
8 cup	64 oz	1895 ml	128	384

Weight

US STANDART	METRIC
1/2 oz	15 g
1 oz	29 g
2 oz	57 g
3 oz	85 g
4 oz	113 g
5 oz	141 g
6 oz	170 g
8 oz	227 g
10 oz	283 g
12 oz	340 g
13 oz	370 g
14 oz	400 g
15 oz	425 g
1 lb	453 g

Temperature

FAHRENHEIT	CELSIUS
100 °F	38°C
150 °F	65 °C
200 °F	93 °C
250 °F	120 °C
300 °F	150 °C
325 °F	160 °C
350 °F	180 °C
375 °F	190 °C
400 °F	200 °C
425 °F	220 °C
450 °F	230 °C
500 °F	260 °C
525 °F	275 °C
550 °F	290 °C

If you want to use your Instant Pot for making delicious and healthy dishes, then let's get started.

The following conventions are used throughout this book:

VEGETARIAN - It means Ovo-Lacto vegetarianism. The dishes include animal/dairy products such as eggs, milk, and honey, but not meat.

VEGAN - The dish does not contain meat, eggs, dairy products, and other animal-derived substances.

GLUTEN-FREE - The dishes exclude gluten, a mixture of proteins found in wheat and related grains, including barley, rye, oat, and all their species and hybrids.

Chapter 1: Breakfast Recipes

<u>Yummy Cobbler Recipe</u>

VEGAN   **VEGETARIAN**   **GLUTEN-FREE**

It is a very simple recipe to enjoy. The cobbler is a very good and effective way to use instant pot, which brings some divine taste to your morning meal.

Servings: 3
Prep Time: 20 minutes
Cook Time: 15 minutes
Pressure Level: High

Ingredients

- 1 pear, peeled and diced
- 2 gala apples, diced
- 4 plums, diced
- 2 tablespoons of brown sugar
- 2 tablespoons of coconut oil
- 3 tablespoons of sunflower seeds
- 1 cup whipping cream, for garnishing
- ½ teaspoon of ground cinnamon
- ½ cup coconut, unsweetened and shredded
- ½ cup pecan, pieces

Directions

1. Put pear, apples, and plums along with brown sugar, cinnamon and coconut oil in an instant pot.
2. Secure the lid of the Instant Pot.
3. Next, close the pressure valve.
4. Select high pressure for 10 minutes.
5. After 10 minutes open the instant Pot and release the steam naturally.
6. Now add pecans, unsweetened coconut, and sunflower seeds into the Instant Pot and press the Sauté button.
7. Let it cook for 5 minutes.
8. Open the Instant Pot, and quick release the steam.
9. Serve it with whipping cream.

Nutrition Facts (Per Serving)

- Calories 721
- Total Fat 61.4g
- Total Carbohydrate 45.1g
- Dietary Fiber 10.6g
- Protein 7.9g

Delicious Breakfast Muffins

VEGETARIAN   **GLUTEN-FREE**

It is a very simple and delicious recipe to enjoy at breakfast. We make the healthy version of this recipe by substitution plain flour with almond meal.

Servings: 4
Prep Time: 20-25 minutes
Cook Time: 12 minutes
Pressure Level: High

Ingredients

- 1 cup almond meal
- 6 tablespoons of raw hemp seeds
- 2 Oz. Parmesan cheese, grated
- 1 tablespoon yeast flakes
- ½ teaspoon baking powder
- ¼ teaspoon of Sea Salt (pinch)
- ½ cup flaxseed meal
- 6 eggs, whisked
- ½ cup green onion, thinly sliced
- ½ cup cottage cheese, low-fat

Directions

1. Take a steamer basket and place it in an instant pot.
2. Add a few cups of water into the instant pot.
3. Take silicon muffin cups and oil spray it.
4. In a large bowl, combine almond meal, hemp seed, flax seed meal, Parmesan cheese, yeast and baking soda.
5. Then add the sea salt.
6. Take a small separate bowl and beat the eggs.
7. Then add cottage cheese and onion to the beaten eggs.
8. Mix the egg mixture to the almond meal bowl.
9. Mix all the ingredients properly.
10. Once all ingredients are combined, fill the silicon muffin cups with the mixture; leave it halfway.
11. Place the muffin cups in steamer according to capacity.
12. Cover the locking lid of the instant pot.
13. Select high pressure for 12 minutes.
14. After 12 minutes, use a quick release.
15. Open the instant Pot and remove muffins from steamer basket.
16. Serve hot and enjoy.

Nutrition Facts (Per Serving)

- Calories 665
- Total Fat 44.5g
- Total Carbohydrate 23.1g
- Dietary Fiber 8.6g
- Protein 43.6g

Bacon with Potatoes

GLUTEN-FREE

It is a simple, healthy and nutritious breakfast that provides all the nutrients essential for your body.

Servings: 4
Prep Time: 15 minutes
Cook Time: 7 minutes
Pressure Level: High

Ingredients

- 2.5 pounds red potatoes, scrubbed and cut into small cubes
- 1.5 cups bacon strips, chopped
- 5 tablespoons of water
- 6 Oz. Cheddar cheese, shredded
- 1 cup Ranch dressing
- 4 teaspoons dried parsley
- ½ teaspoon sea salt
- 3 teaspoons garlic powder

Directions

1. Add bacon, potatoes with water into the instant pot.
2. Stir in sea salt, parsley, and garlic powder.
3. Set pressure to high and cook for 7 minutes.
4. Once timer beeps, open the instant pot.
5. Now add the cheese and ranch dressing to the pot and stir few times.
6. The heat will melt the cheese.
7. Serve immediately.
8. Enjoy.

Nutrition Facts (Per Serving)

- Calories 433
- Total Fat 18.1g
- Total Carbohydrate 50.5g
- Dietary Fiber 5.2g
- Protein 18.6g

Breakfast Quinoa

VEGETARIAN   **GLUTEN-FREE**

If you love porridge and need a healthy alternative, then try this recipe, as we are using quinoa instead of oats to make it low calorie and a much healthier breakfast to enjoy.

Servings: 2
Prep Time: 2 minutes
Cook Time: 2 minutes
Pressure Level: High

Ingredients

- 2 cups quinoa, uncooked
- 2 cups of water
- 2 tablespoons sugar
- ½ teaspoon cinnamon, ground
- Sea salt, pinch
- 1 cup low-fat milk
- ¼ teaspoon vanilla bean

Directions

1 Take an instant pot and add quinoa along with water, sugar, vanilla bean, salt, and cinnamon.
2 Select high pressure and cook for 1 minute.
3 When the instant pot timer beeps, turn it off.
4 Open the pot after using quick release.
5 Add in milk and stir to combine.
6 Close the pot and cook it on high for one more minute.
7 Then serve hot.

Nutrition Facts (Per Serving)

- Calories 736
- Total Fat 11.9g
- Total Carbohydrate 129.5g
- Dietary Fiber 12.2g
- Protein 28.5g

Plain Boiled Egg

VEGETARIAN   **GLUTEN-FREE**

It is a very simple and light egg recipe to enjoy. It is the best recipe to enjoy a snack.

Servings: 6
Prep Time: 15 minutes
Cook Time: 5 minutes
Pressure Level: High

Ingredients

- 6 Pasture-raised eggs
- 1 cup water
- 1 tsp Paprika
- Salt, to taste

Directions

1. Plug the instant pot and pour one cup of water in the instant pot.
2. Place a steamer basket in the instant pot.
3. Place eggs on the top of the steamer basket.
4. Cover and adjust the time 5 minutes at high pressure.
5. When the instant pot timer beeps, turn it off.
6. Use a quick pressure release.
7. Remove and peel the eggs.
8. Slice in half and sprinkle salt and paprika.
9. Serve it immediately.

Nutrition Facts (Per Serving)

- Calories 71
- Total Fat 4.5 g
- Total Carbohydrate 1.2g
- Dietary Fiber 0.1g
- Protein 6.1g

Classic Porridge

VEGAN   **VEGETARIAN**   **GLUTEN-FREE**

It is a classic breakfast porridge that is loved by the whole family. The added richness of blueberries and strawberries makes it a great meal for breakfast.

Servings: 2
Prep Time: 10 minutes
Cook Time: 8 minutes
Pressure Level: High

Ingredients

- 1 cup raw cashews, pre-soaked
- ½ cup pecan, about 10 pieces
- ½ cup shredded dry coconut, unsweetened
- 2 tablespoons of coconut oil, melted
- 2 teaspoons of brown sugar
- 1 cup oats
- 1 cup water

Side serving

- 1/3 cup blueberries
- ½ cup strawberries, chopped

Directions

1. Combine cashews, pecans, coconut, water, brown sugar, and coconut oil in a blender and pulse it until a smooth consistency is obtained.
2. Transfer the content to the instant pot.
3. Next, add the oats to the instant pot.
4. Select high pressure for 8 minutes.
5. Close the lid of the pot and press the Porridge button.
6. Once timer beeps, release the pressure naturally.
7. Stir the porridge and serve with blueberries and strawberries.

Nutrition Facts (Per Serving)

- Calories 777
- Total Fat 55.3g
- Total Carbohydrate 62.4g
- Dietary Fiber 9.3g
- Protein 17 g

Best Scrambled Eggs

VEGETARIAN   **GLUTEN-FREE**

Everyone loves scrambled eggs, and to make it even quicker, we have introduced this recipe that is simply loaded with good fat and a lot of protein.

Servings: 4
Prep Time: 10 minutes
Cook Time: 7 minutes
Pressure Level: Low

Ingredients

- 5 eggs
- 2 tablespoons of butter, melted
- Salt and black pepper, to taste
- 2 tablespoons of almond milk

Directions

1 Oil sprays a heatproof bowl.
2 Add milk, butter, salt and black pepper to the bowl.
3 Beat eggs in a small separate and add it to the milk.
4 Pour two cups of water in the Instant Pot.
5 Then fit the trivet in a pot.
6 Set the heatproof bowl on the top of the trivet.
7 Close the pot and select low pressure for 7 minutes.
8 After 7 minutes, quick release steam.
9 Serve hot.
10 Enjoy.

Nutrition Facts (Per Serving)

- Calories 118
- Total Fat 10.4g
- Total Carbohydrate 0.7g
- Dietary Fiber 0.1g
- Protein 5.7g

Fruity Bread

VEGETARIAN   GLUTEN-FREE

The hit combination of bananas and avocado make it a surprising delicious bread to enjoy as breakfast.

Servings: 6
Prep Time: 15 minutes
Cook Time: 20 minutes
Pressure Level: High

Ingredients

- 4 cups almond flour
- 6 tablespoons grapeseed oil
- 1 teaspoon vanilla extract
- 4 tablespoons sugar
- 2-3 organic eggs
- 1 cup banana, mashed
- 2 teaspoons baking powder
- ¼ teaspoon salt
- 1 large cup avocado, pitted and mashed
- Oil spray, for greasing

Directions

1. Take a medium or small push pan and grease it with oil spray.
2. Take a bowl and mix flour, salt, and soda.
3. Blend oil, sugar and mashed avocados, eggs, bananas, vanilla extract in a blender until smooth.
4. Combine wet ingredients with dry ingredients.
5. Pour this mixture in to push pan.
6. Place trivet in the instant pot and add a few cups of water.
7. Make a sling of aluminum foil and place it on the trivet.
8. Place push pan on top of foil.
9. Close the pot and cook it on high pressure for 20 -22 minutes.
10. Then use a quick release method to release the steam.
11. Serve the bread, cool down once.

Nutrition Facts (Per Serving)

- Calories 481
- Total Fat 43.4g
- Total Carbohydrate 20.8g
- Dietary Fiber 4.4g
- Protein 6.6g

Marvelous Pancakes

VEGETARIAN   **GLUTEN-FREE**

These breakfast pancakes are simple to make, yet they taste divine. Once you take a bit of it, you will surely ask for more.

Servings: 4
Prep Time: 25 minutes
Cook Time: 20 minutes
Pressure Level: Low

Ingredients

- 2 cups almond flour
- 2 teaspoons baking powder
- 2 large eggs
- 1 to 1½ coconut or plain milk
- 1 cup maple syrup
- 2 tablespoons of brown sugar

Directions

1 Take a bowl and whisked eggs in it.
2 Then add in baking powder, milk, sugar, and flour.
3 Grease the bottom of the instant pot with oil spray.
4 Pour the mixture into the pot.
5 Close the pot and program it to manual mode.
6 Set pressure to low.
7 Set the cooking time to 20 minutes.
8 Once timer beeps, quick release the steam.
9 Open the instant pot and loosen the pancake with the help of spatula from the sides and bottom.
10 Serve with a drizzle of maple syrup.

Nutrition Facts (Per Serving)

- Calories 696
- Total Fat 42.5g
- Total Carbohydrate 76.7g
- Dietary Fiber 10.5g
- Protein 9.5g

Chapter 2: Delicious Vegetable Recipes

Garden Stew

VEGAN   **VEGETARIAN**

It is a simple yet delicious stew that is low in calories as well. The combination of potatoes, cauliflower, and mushroom make it a perfectly tasty meal to enjoy.

Please note couscous contains gluten! If you have gluten intolerance, replace couscous with corn or rice.

Servings: 4
Prep Time: 20 minutes
Cook Time: 7 minutes
Pressure Level: High

Ingredients

- 3 cups vegetable broth
- 2 bay leaves
- 2 small zucchinis, sliced
- Salt and pepper, to taste
- 2 Oz. Sliced Shiitake mushrooms, chopped
- 4 Oz. Cauliflowers, florets
- 2 sweet potatoes, peeled and cubed
- 4 red onions, cut into wedges
- 1 cup of sweet tomato
- 2 cloves garlic, minced
- 2 teaspoons, dried savory leaves
- 2 -3 cups cooked couscous, warm, for serve

Directions

1 Combine all the listed ingredients in an instant pot (except cooked couscous).
2 Cover the pot and adjust the cooking time to 7-10 minutes at high pressure.
3 After 15 minutes, release the steam naturally.
4 Serve the cooked stew with cooked couscous.

Nutrition Facts (Per Serving)

- Calories 210
- Total Fat 0.7g
- Total Carbohydrate 42.9g
- Dietary Fiber 4.2g
- Protein 7.8g

Mix Veggies

VEGETARIAN   **GLUTEN-FREE**

You are just 15 minutes away from making this nutritious risotto dish that accompanies some finest ingredients that keep you satisfied and fill your body with energy.

Servings: 4
Prep Time: 25 minutes
Cook Time: 15 minutes
Pressure Level: High

Ingredients

- 1 white onion, diced
- 4 tablespoons vegetable oil
- Salt, to taste
- 2 garlic cloves
- ⅓ Cup white wine vinegar
- 2 fennels, diced
- 1 cup asparagus, diced
- 2 cups vegetable stock
- 4 tablespoons of organic butter
- 1 cup Parmesan cheese, grated

Ingredients for toppings

- 2 tablespoons olive oil
- 1 fennel
- 1 asparagus, cubed
- ¼ teaspoon salt
- ½ lemon, juice only

Directions

1. Pour vegetable oil in an instant pot and press sauté button.
2. Add in the onion and garlic.
3. Cook for 2 minutes.
4. Then add fennel and asparagus along with a salt, vinegar, and stock.
5. Lock the lid of the instant pot.
6. Select High Pressure and set a timer to 7 minutes.
7. Once the timer beeps, let the steam release naturally.

Prepare Toppings by Using Topping Ingredients

1. Meanwhile, take a non-stick skillet and heat olive oil in the pan.
2. Add fennel, asparagus, salt and lemon juice to the pan and cook for a few minutes.
3. Open the pot and dump in the butter and cheese.
4. Stir to combine well and then top it with pan ingredients.
5. Serve and enjoy.

Nutrition Facts (Per Serving)

- Calories 444
- Total Fat 37.6g
- Total Carbohydrate 19.2g
- Dietary Fiber 7.3g
- Protein 9.9g

Coconut and Cabbage for Lunch

VEGAN   **VEGETARIAN**   **GLUTEN-FREE**

The richness of coconut milk makes this recipe not only healthy but also a mouthwatering lunch to enjoy.

Servings: 4

Prep Time: 15-20 minutes

Cook Time: 10 minutes

Pressure Level: High

Ingredients

- 2 tablespoons olive oil
- 1 red onion, halved and sliced
- 1 teaspoon salt
- 2 garlic cloves, diced
- 1 cup carrot, peeled and sliced
- 2 tablespoons lemon juice
- ½ Cup unsweetened coconut milk
- 1 red chili, sliced
- 2 tablespoons mustard seeds
- 1 tablespoon curry powder
- 1/3 tablespoon turmeric powder
- 2 cups cabbage, shredded or sliced (core removed)
- ½ Cup water

Directions

1. Press sauté button of instant Pot and sauté onion in olive oil for 4 minutes.
2. Then start adding salt, garlic, red chili, mustard seeds, curry powder, turmeric powder, cabbage, carrots, lemon juice, and water.

3   Press the Warm button of the instant pot and lock the lid.
4   Set timer for 5 minutes at high pressure.
5   After 5 minutes do a quick release to let the steam escape.
6   Add coconut milk.
7   Stir it for few times and then serve.

Nutrition Facts (Per Serving)

- Calories 200
- Total Fat 16.2g
- Total Carbohydrate 13.5g
- Dietary Fiber 4.6g
- Protein 3.6g

Best Vegetable Casserole

VEGETARIAN　　　　**GLUTEN-FREE**

Zucchini is a part of the recipe that is rich in fiber, vitamins, protein, magnesium, and folate. Zucchinis cooked very nicely and quickly in instant pot, making it an easy recipe to prepare.

Servings: 4
Prep Time: 15 minutes
Cook Time: 5 minutes
Pressure Level: High

Ingredients

- 2 large red onions, peeled and sliced
- 2 green bell peppers cut into strips
- 1 large zucchini, peeled and sliced
- 1 cup red tomatoes, diced
- 4 tablespoons butter
- ½ cup Parmesan cheese, grated
- 2 tablespoons of water
- 2 cups boiled rice, side servings
- Salt, to taste
- Freshly grounded black pepper, to taste

Directions

1 Combine onions, bell peppers, tomatoes, zucchini, salt, and pepper in an instant pot along with 2 tablespoons of water.
2 Cook on high for 5 minutes.
3 Afterward, open the pot by the quick release method.
4 Now add butter and cheese.
5 Stir for 2 minutes.
6 Serve with the cook boiled rice and enjoy.

Nutrition Facts (Per Serving)

- Calories 612
- Total Fat 15.6g
- Total Carbohydrate 103.5g
- Dietary Fiber 9.5g
- Protein 17.4g

Mixed Vegetable Recipe

VEGETARIAN

It is a very simple, hearty and delicious meal that makes it easy for you to alter veggies of your preference.

Servings: 6
Prep Time: 20 minutes
Cook Time: 15 minutes
Pressure Level: High

Ingredients
- 2 cups carrot, cubed
- 1 cup corn
- 1 cup turnip, peeled and cubed
- 1 can cream of mushroom soup
- Salt, to taste
- Pepper, to taste
- 1 cup zucchini, cubed
- 1 bell pepper, cubed
- 1/3 tablespoon garlic powder
- ½ teaspoon of ginger

Directions
1. Place all the ingredients in an instant pot.
2. Set timer for 15 minutes at high.
3. Use the quick release to let the steam escape.
4. Serve hot and enjoy.

Nutrition Facts (Per Serving)
- Calories 144
- Total Fat 4.9g
- Total Carbohydrate 23.5g
- Dietary Fiber 3.8g
- Protein 3.9g

Sweet and Tangy Beetroots

VEGAN   VEGETARIAN   GLUTEN-FREE

This recipe gets its tang from the apple cider vinegar and sweetness from the brown sugar. Honey can also be used as an alternative to sugar. This recipe is best served with steamed rice.

Servings: 4

Prep Time: 18 minutes

Cook Time: 12 minutes

Pressure Level: High

Ingredients

- 1 cup brown sugar
- ½ cup of water
- ½ cup Apple cider vinegar
- 2 cups of whole beets, canned and drained
- 2 tablespoons almond flour

Directions

1. Take a bowl, mix together sugar, flour, apple cider vinegar, and water.
2. Dump it in an instant pot.
3. Next, add in the Beetroots.
4. Set the cooking time to 12 minutes at high.
5. Use the quick release to let the steam escape.
6. Serve hot.

Nutrition Facts (Per Serving)

- Calories 167
- Total Fat 0.8g
- Total Carbohydrate 38.7g
- Dietary Fiber 1.2g
- Protein 0.9g

Hearty and Divine Chowder

VEGAN　　　**VEGETARIAN**　　　**GLUTEN-FREE**

After making this chowder what you will get is a creamy, hot, and divine taste and texture that is filled with the goodness of most healthy nutrient dense vegetables.

Servings: 4
Prep Time: 25 minutes
Cook Time: 14 minutes
Pressure Level: High

Ingredients

- 2 cups fat-free vegetable broth
- 2 large sweet potatoes, peeled and cubed
- 2 cups kernel corn, whole
- 1 cup coconut milk, divided
- 2 tablespoons cornstarch
- Salt and pepper, to taste
- 2 tablespoons of water
- 2 red onions, chopped
- 1 cup celery, sliced
- 2 teaspoons dried thyme leaves

Directions

1. Combine vegetable broth, sweet potatoes, corn kernels, red onions, celery, thyme, salt, and black pepper in an instant pot.
2. Close the pot and set the timer for 12 minutes at high.
3. Afterward, natural release the steam.
4. Open the pot and add in the coconut milk, and cook it for 2 minutes.
5. Meanwhile, mix cornstarch in water.
6. Open the instant pot and add in the cornstarch mixture.
7. Cook for 2 more minutes.
8. Serve.

Nutrition Facts (Per Serving)

- Calories 328
- Total Fat 15.4g
- Total Carbohydrate 47g
- Dietary Fiber 7.2g
- Protein 5.7g

Creamy and Cheesy Soup

VEGETARIAN

A recipe packed with the goodness of broccoli and the cheesiness of cottage cheese.

Servings: 6
Prep Time: 20 minutes
Cook Time: 10 minutes
Pressure Level: High

Ingredients

- 2 cups frozen broccoli, washed
- 2 cups cauliflower, washed and thawed
- 2 cups carrot, sliced
- 1 cup chopped onion
- 2 cups cottage cheese
- Pepper, to taste
- Salt, to taste
- Cooking spray, for greasing
- 2 cans cream of mushroom soup,
- 3 ounces chopped pimientos, drained

Directions

1 Grease the bottom of the instant pot with oil spray.

2 Combine the entire ingredient in an instant pot and set the timer for 10 minutes at high pressure.

3 After 10 minutes, quick release the steam.

4 Serve hot.

Nutrition Facts (Per Serving)

- Calories 212
- Total Fat 7.5
- Total Carbohydrate 22.9g
- Dietary Fiber 3.7g
- Protein 14.5g

Chapter 3: Delicious Soups

<u>Yummy Mushroom Soup</u>

VEGETARIAN

It is easy to make soup, and it offers a deep rich taste. It presents the pure essence of mushroom.

Servings: 6
Prep Time: 20 minutes
Cook Time: 10 minutes
Pressure Level: High

Ingredients

- 4 cups chicken or vegetable stock
- 1 cup celery, sliced
- ½ cup baby carrots
- 2 medium white onions, peeled and chopped
- ½ cup pearl barley
- 14 Oz. Dried mushrooms, chopped
- Salt and white pepper, to taste
- 1/3 cup sour cream

Directions

1 Combine stock, onions, celery, baby carrots, pearl barley, and mushroom, salt, and pepper in an instant pot.
2 Close the pot and set time to 10 minutes at high pressure.
3 Afterward, release the pressure by a quick release method.
4 Serve the soup into a bowl and garnish with a dollop of sour cream.
5 Enjoy hot.

Nutrition Facts (Per Serving)

- Calories 332
- Total Fat 7.4g
- Total Carbohydrate 20.3g
- Dietary Fiber 4.6g
- Protein 45.2g

Summertime Soup

GLUTEN-FREE

It is a dense and thick soup with tons of mouthwatering flours. It is super easy and a great way to use squash and an instant pot make all the things done so easily.

Servings: 6
Prep Time: 25 minutes
Cook Time: 14 minutes
Pressure Level: High

Ingredients

- 2 tablespoons of olive oil
- 4 cups chicken stock
- ½ cup zucchini, sliced
- 2 white onions, chopped
- 2 cloves garlic, minced
- 1 cup of diced tomatoes
- 1 cup of green beans
- ½ cup of carrot, chopped
- 2 cups chopped butternut squash, peeled and seedless
- 2 teaspoons Worcestershire sauce
- 2 teaspoons dried rosemary leaves
- Salt and freshly grounded black pepper, to taste

Directions

1 Press sauté button of instant pot and sauté onion along with olive oil for few minutes.
2 After 2 minutes, add the pepper, salt, and garlic.
3 Then add tomatoes and cook for 2 more minutes.
4 At this stage put all the remaining listed ingredients one by one.
5 Close the instant pot and set the timer for 10 minutes at high pressure.
6 After 15 minutes, let the pressure release naturally.
7 Serve the soup into a bowl and enjoy.

Nutrition Facts (Per Serving)

- Calories 167
- Total Fat 10.4g
- Total Carbohydrate 19g
- Dietary Fiber 3.9g
- Total Sugars 6.1g
- Protein 3g

Simple Lentils Spinach Soup

VEGAN   **VEGETARIAN**   **GLUTEN-FREE**

It is a very rich and vibrant green soup, that's healthy and filling at the same time.

Servings: 6
Prep Time: 20 minutes
Cook Time: 12 minutes
Pressure Level: High

Ingredients

- 6 cups vegetable broth
- ½ cup tomatoes, undrained
- 2 cups chopped spinach, thawed and drained
- Salt and black pepper, to taste
- 1/3 cup carrot
- 2 large cloves garlic, minced
- 1/3 cup dried brown lentils
- 1 onion, peeled and chopped
- ¼ cup celery
- ½ teaspoon chili powder
- 1 teaspoon curry powder

Directions

1. Combine all ingredients in an instant pot.
2. Set timer for 12 minutes at high pressure.
3. After 12 minutes, let the pressure release naturally.
4. Serve in soup bowls and enjoy.

Nutrition Facts (Per Serving)

- Calories 81
- Total Fat 1.3g
- Total Carbohydrate 11g
- Dietary Fiber 2.4g
- Protein 6.7g

Spicy and Yummy Soup

VEGAN   **VEGETARIAN**

It is a very light, simple, and low-fat soup that maintains your health in an effective way.

Servings: 6
Prep Time: 20 minutes
Cook Time: 16 minutes
Pressure Level: High

Ingredients

- 3 cups of vegetable broth
- 1 teaspoon thyme leaves
- Salt, to taste
- Freshly grounded black pepper
- ½ cup carrot
- ½ cup celery
- 2-4 tablespoons tomato paste
- ¼ cup pearl barley
- 3 cups water
- 1 cup turnip
- 1 large clove garlic, minced
- 2 bay leaves
- 1 teaspoon dried marjoram leaves
- 1 cup onion, chopped
- 1 cup sliced mushrooms

Directions

1. Combine all the listed ingredients in an instant pot.
2. Set timer for 15 minutes at high pressure.
3. After 15 minutes, let the pressure release naturally.
4. Let the soup get cooled down.
5. Take a blender and blend the soup until a smooth consistency is obtained.
6. Again transfer the soup in an instant pot and cook for 1 more minutes at high pressure, just to make it hot.
7. Serve into soup bowls and enjoy.

Nutrition Facts (Per Serving)

- Calories 82
- Total Fat 1g
- Total Carbohydrate 14.3g
- Dietary Fiber 3.4g
- Protein 4.9g

Exquisite Chicken and Vegetable Soup

GLUTEN-FREE

It is a recipe that it's not only delicious, but also full of nutrients like minerals, protein, calcium, and fiber.

Servings: 6
Prep Time: 20 minutes
Cook Time: 12 minutes
Pressure Level: High

Ingredients

- 6 cups chicken broth
- 2 cups cabbage, coarsely shredded
- ½ cup onion, chopped
- 1 cup dry red wine
- 1 pound chicken meat, cubed and boneless
- 1 cup Chickpea, rinsed, drained
- ½ cup leeks, chopped
- ½ cup turnip
- 2 cloves garlic, chopped
- 1 teaspoon of ginger
- 1 teaspoon dried thyme leaves
- Salt and pepper, to taste

Directions

1. Combine all ingredients in an instant pot.
2. Adjust the timer to 12 minutes at high pressure.
3. After 12 minutes, let the pressure release naturally.
4. Serve and enjoy.

Nutrition Facts (Per Serving)

- Calories 356
- Total Fat 9.1g
- Total Carbohydrate 26.8g
- Dietary Fiber 7g
- Protein 33.9g

Hot Chicken Soup

GLUTEN-FREE

The seasoning combined in this easy chicken noodle soup recipe makes it a mouthwatering experience to enjoy.

Servings: 6
Prep Time: 20 minutes
Cook Time: 14 minutes
Pressure Level: High

Ingredients

- 6 cups Chicken Stock
- 1 teaspoon of ginger and garlic paste
- 2 tablespoons of olive oil
- 2 pounds boneless, skinless chicken breast, thinly sliced
- 1 cup onion, coarsely chopped
- 1 cup celery
- ½ cup almond meal
- 1/3 teaspoon ground cloves
- Salt and black pepper, to taste
- Handful of Thyme leaves
- 1 teaspoon of red chili flakes
- 1 cup stewed tomatoes

Directions

1. Press the sautéed button of instant pot and place onions on it along with oil.
2. Sauté the onion for 2 minutes, then add ginger and garlic.
3. Let it cook for one minute and add chicken pieces and tomatoes.
4. Let it cook for a minute and add all the remaining listed ingredients.
5. Close the instant pot and set the timer for 10 minutes at high pressure.
6. Then open the pot by the quick release method.
7. Serve.

Nutrition Facts (Per Serving)

- Calories 283
- Total Fat 12.9g
- Total Carbohydrate 6.1g
- Dietary Fiber 2.1g
- Protein 34.9g

Noodles in Chicken soup

A very easy noodles recipe that took just a few minutes to prepare. The mushrooms add extra nutrition to the recipe.

Servings: 6
Prep Time: 15 minutes
Cook Time: 25 minutes
Pressure Level: High

Ingredients

- ½ cup Shiitake mushrooms
- 2 cups hot boiling water
- Salt and black pepper, to taste
- 2 cups dried chow mein noodles
- 1 cup carrots
- 2 teaspoons light soy sauce
- 1 cup boneless chicken breast, cubed
- ½ cup white mushrooms
- 6 cups Chicken broth
- 3 tablespoons dry sherry
- 1 teaspoon five-spice powder
- 1 cup Snow peas, trimmed

Directions

1. Pour hot water into a bowl and add shiitake mushrooms, let it sit for 10 minutes, then drain the water.
2. Place shiitake mushrooms, chicken broth, chicken breast pieces, dry sherry, white mushrooms, carrots, soy sauce, five spice powder, snow peas, salt and black pepper in instant pot.
3. Close the pot and set a timer for 10 minutes at high pressure.
4. After 10 minutes, open the pot by releasing steam using the quick release method.
5. Add chow mein noodles to pot.
6. Now close the pot.
7. Set the timer for 5-6 minutes.
8. Keep pressure low.
9. Let the steam release naturally, and then open the pot.
10. Serve the soup into a bowl and enjoy.

Nutrition Facts (Per Serving)

- Calories 220
- Total Fat 7.8g
- Total Carbohydrate 15.7g
- Dietary Fiber 2.5g
- Protein 14.4g

Cheesy Easy Broccoli Soup

GLUTEN-FREE

There is nothing more flavorful and better than a bowl of broccoli soup served with bread. It is a hit winter time soup to enjoy.

Servings: 6
Prep Time: 16 minutes
Cook Time: 9 minutes
Pressure Level: High

Ingredients

- 3 cups broccoli florets
- 1 tablespoon of olive oil
- 1 tablespoon of garlic paste
- Salt, to taste
- Black pepper, to taste
- 1 teaspoon of ginger paste
- 2 white onions, chopped
- 4 cups chicken bone broth with ginger
- 2 cups grated cheddar cheese
- 1 cup heavy cream

Directions

1. Sauté the onions, along with oil in an instant pot by pressing sauté button.
2. Open the instant pot and add all the remaining ingredients excluding the cream and cheese.
3. Close pot and press manual mode for 5 minutes at high pressure.
4. After 5 minutes, let the steam release naturally.
5. Then serve soup into the bowl with cheese and cream on top.
6. Enjoy immediately.

Nutrition Facts (Per Serving)

- Calories 85.6
- Total Fat 3.73
- Total Carbohydrate 1.36g
- Dietary Fiber 0.35g
- Protein 10.9g

Chapter 4: Meat and Poultry

<u>Perfect Chicken Adobo</u>

GLUTEN-FREE

An authentic Filipino dish is prepared with vinegar and soy sauce in just 15 minutes using instant pot. Once you have a bit of it, you will ask for more.

Servings: 6
Prep Time: 20 minutes
Cook Time: 15 minutes
Pressure Level: High

Ingredients

- 2 pounds chicken meat
- 2-4 tablespoons olive oil
- 2 tablespoons fish sauce
- 2 tablespoons brown sugar
- 1/3 cup vinegar (*I recommend Apple Cider Vinegar*)
- ½ teaspoon ground black peppercorn
- 4 cloves garlic
- 1/3 cup soy sauce
- 4 tablespoons of light soy sauce

Directions

1. Take a bowl and whisk together peppercorn, soy sauce, light soy sauce, vinegar, sugar and fish sauce.
2. Now, add olive oil to the instant pot and turn on the sauté button.
3. Add the chicken and garlic to the pot and cook 3 minutes.
4. Next, remove chicken from the pot.
5. Dump the bowl mixture to the pot and cook on high pressure for a minute.
6. Add the chicken and de-glaze the instant pot.
7. Cook for 10 minutes at high pressure than natural release.
8. Serve and enjoy.

Nutrition Facts (Per Serving)

- Calories 392
- Total Fat 20.5g
- Total Carbohydrate 4.8g
- Dietary Fiber 0g
- Protein 45g

Instant Pot Roast

It is a simple recipe, which brings some divine taste to your dinner table in no time. The instant pot doesn't let the flavors escape, and you end up with a tender roast.

Servings: 4
Prep Time: 50 minutes
Cook Time: 20 minutes
Pressure Level: High

Ingredients

- 2 pounds beef
- 2 tablespoons salad dressing mix
- ½ cup ranch dressing mix, dry
- ½ cup brown gravy mix
- 1 cup water

Directions

1. Combine all the listed ingredients in a bowl and rub over the meat well.
2. Let the beef marinate for 30 minutes.
3. Place the beef along with gravy in the instant pot and cook on high pressure for 20 minutes.
4. Then release naturally.
5. Serve and enjoy.

Nutrition Facts (Per Serving)

- Calories 974
- Total Fat 57.4g
- Total Carbohydrate 33.8g
- Dietary Fiber 7.3g
- Protein 83.5g

<u>Ginger Chicken</u>

GLUTEN-FREE

In this recipe, we marinate the chicken wings in sweet and sticky soy glaze for perfect taste.

Servings: 6
Prep Time: 20 minutes
Cook Time: 14 minutes
Pressure Level: High

Ingredients

- 2 pounds chicken wings, disjointed
- 2 tablespoons ginger, minced
- 2 cloves garlic, minced
- 2 tablespoons of five-spice powders
- ½ cup soy sauce *(may contain a gluten!)*
- 2 tablespoons brown sugar

Directions

1. Combine soy sauce, brown sugar, minced ginger, minced garlic and five spice powders in a large bowl.
2. Mix the bowl ingredients well.
3. Rub this mixture over the chicken wings.
4. Next, place trivet inside a pot and pour 2 cups of water.
5. Then place the chicken wings on top of the trivet.
6. Press the meat stew button to turn on the instant pot.
7. Cook at high pressure for 12 minutes.
8. Naturally, release the steam.
9. Preheat the oven to 400° F.
10. Finish wings in the oven for baking it for about 10-12 minutes.
11. Serve.

Nutrition Facts (Per Serving)

- Calories 320
- Total Fat 11.3g
- Total Carbohydrate 6.3g
- Dietary Fiber 0.8g
- Protein 45.5g

Beetroot Stew

GLUTEN-FREE

It is a very delicious and hearty dish to enjoy. The beetroots go very well with the boiled rice.

Servings: 6
Prep Time: 25 minutes
Cook Time: 20 minutes
Pressure Level: High

Ingredients
- 2 cups Beetroots, peeled and cubed
- 2 pounds cubed beef, boneless
- 2 cups boiled rice
- 2 cups beef broth
- 2 tablespoons red chilies
- Black pepper, to taste
- Salt, to taste

Directions
1. Dump all the listed ingredients in an instant pot and cook for about 20-22 minutes at high pressure.
2. Quickly release the steam.
3. Serve with boiled rice.

Nutrition Facts (Per Serving)

- Calories 557
- Total Fat 12.5g
- Total Carbohydrate 55.8g
- Dietary Fiber 2.2g
- Protein 51.2g

Chicken in Best Gravy

GLUTEN-FREE

The addition of brown sugar adds extra flavor to the gravy making the recipe a mouth-watering experience.

Servings: 6
Prep Time: 25 minutes
Cook Time: 15 minutes
Pressure Level: High

Ingredients

- 4 pounds chicken, boneless and leg pieces
- 2 tablespoons ketchup *(May contain a gluten!)*
- 4 tablespoons dark brown sugar
- 2 cloves garlic, crushed
- Salt and freshly ground black pepper, to taste
- 2 teaspoons ground ginger
- ½ cup soy sauce *(May contain a gluten!)*

Directions

1 Take an instant pot and place all the ingredients in it.
2 Press the meat stew button to turn on the instant pot.
3 Cook for about 15 minutes at high.
4 Once done, serve and enjoy.

Nutrition Facts (Per Serving)

- Calories 499
- Total Fat 9.2g
- Total Carbohydrate 9.5g
- Dietary Fiber 0.3g
- Protein 89.2g

Beef with Dried Apricots

GLUTEN-FREE

A unique dish that is easily made and can be served over baked potatoes or boiled rice. The hint of cinnamon makes the recipe divine in taste.

Servings: 6
Prep Time: 25 minutes
Cook Time: 20 minutes
Pressure Level: High

Ingredients

- 2 large red onions, thinly sliced
- 1 tablespoon cumin, ground
- 1 teaspoon of nutmeg
- 2 cups dried apricots
- 1 cup dry red wine
- 1 teaspoon cinnamon, ground
- 2 teaspoons garlic powder
- Salt and black pepper, to taste
- 1 teaspoon coriander, ground
- 2 cups beef stock
- 2 parsnips, chopped
- 2 pounds beef brisket, boneless

Directions

1. Take an instant and place onion and parsnip in the bottom.
2. Take a bowl and mix the nutmeg, garlic, salt, pepper, cinnamon, coriander, and cumin in it.
3. Rub the bowl spices over the beef.
4. Layer parsnip and onion on the bottom of instant pot
5. Now add the beef on top of the parsnip inside the pot.
6. Now top the meat with apricots, wine, and stock.
7. Press the meat stew button and cook on high pressure for 20 minutes.
8. Once done, serve.

Nutrition Facts (Per Serving)

- Calories 440
- Total Fat 10.6g
- Total Carbohydrate 29g
- Dietary Fiber 6.9g
- Protein 49.5g

Divine Instant Ribs

GLUTEN-FREE

It is a very easy dish, which can be prepared to quick start your cooking journey in instant pot. Just grab your BBQ sauce and we are good to go.

Servings: 4
Prep Time: 55 minutes
Cook Time: 25 minutes
Pressure Level: High

Ingredients

- 1.5 pounds of baby back ribs
- Black pepper, to taste
- 2-4 tablespoons BBQ sauce
- Salt, to taste

Directions

1 Preheat the oven to 450°F.
2 First, wash the ribs and remove the membranes from the ribs.
3 Season the ribs with salt, pepper and BBQ sauce.
4 Let it sit for 30 minutes.
5 Now place the trivet into the instant pot and pour 2 cups of water.
6 Put the marinated ribs on top of the trivet.
7 Close the instant pot lid and cook at high pressure for 15 minutes.
8 Next, release the steam naturally.
9 Open the lid of the instant pot.
10 Finish it in the oven for about 10 minutes.
11 Serve and enjoy.

Nutrition Facts (Per Serving)

- Calories 403
- Total Fat 20.8g
- Total Carbohydrate 5.7g
- Dietary Fiber 0.1g
- Protein 44.8g

Steak with Gravy

GLUTEN-FREE

It is a perfect steak recipe to enjoy at lunch or even dinner time.

The almond flour is added as an alternative to plain flour.

Servings: 6
Prep Time: 30 minutes
Cook Time: 26 minutes
Pressure Level: High

Ingredients

- 2 pounds steak, cubed
- Salt and black pepper, to taste
- 4 tablespoons of onion gravy mix
- ½ cup Almond flour, for dredging
- 1 can cream of mushroom soup
- 2 cups water
- 2 tablespoons of olive oil

Directions

1. Season the steak with salt and pepper and then dredge in the almond flour.
2. Turn on the sauté mode of the instant pot.
3. Add oil to the pot and cook steak for 1 minute at high pressure.
4. Afterward, open the pot and add the remaining ingredients to the pot.
5. Press the meat stew button to turn on the instant Pot and set a timer for 25 minutes.
6. Quickly release the steam.
7. Serve hot.
8. Enjoy.

Nutrition Facts (Per Servings)

- Calories 408
- Total Fat 16.5g
- Total Carbohydrate 5.4g
- Dietary Fiber 0.3g
- Protein 56.5g

Chapter 5: Fish and Seafood's

Classic Shrimp Stew

GLUTEN-FREE

Some delicious and nutritious vegetables are part of the recipe that takes it to another level.

Servings: 5
Prep Time: 20 minutes
Cook Time: 10 minutes
Pressure Level: Low

Ingredients

- 2 cups tomatoes, stew
- 2 ounces turkey sausage, thickly sliced
- ½ cup baby carrot
- 1 cup Brussels sprouts
- 1 cup kernel corn
- 2 -3 white onions cut into thin wedges
- 2 teaspoons chili powder
- 6 ounces shrimp, peeled
- Salt and freshly grounded black pepper, to taste

Directions

1. Place all the listed ingredients in an instant pot.
2. Cook it on low pressure for 10 minutes.
3. Open the pot by the quick release method.
4. Transfer the stew into the serving bowls and enjoy.
5. Serve.

Nutrition Facts (Per Serving)

- Calories 159
- Total Fat 4.6g
- Total Carbohydrate 18.4g
- Dietary Fiber 4.7g
- Protein 13g

Pasta with Mixed Seafood

A simple and classic pasta recipe, that is rich in some intense flavors. We have introduced mixed seafood to make it rich in omega-3.

Servings: 5
Prep Time: 25 minutes
Cook Time: 10 minutes
Pressure Level: High

Ingredients

- ½ cup dry white wine
- 2 Oz. Crab meat, sliced
- 2 Oz. Haddock steak, cubed
- 1 cup mushrooms
- 2 cloves garlic, minced
- 1 tablespoon tomato paste
- 1 teaspoon oregano
- 1 teaspoon basil leaves, crumbled
- 1 oz. pasta, cooked
- 1 teaspoon turmeric powder
- 1 oz. Sea scallops or any seafood
- Salt and pepper, to taste
- 1 cup chopped tomatoes
- ½ cup red bell pepper, onion,

Directions

1 First, cook pasta according to the package instructions.
2 Meanwhile, place all remaining ingredients in an instant pot and cook at high pressure for 10 minutes.
3 Once cooked, naturally release the steam.
4 Serve it over the cooked fettuccine.

Nutrition Facts (Per Serving)

- Calories 265
- Total Fat 2.3g
- Total Carbohydrate 38.4g
- Dietary Fiber 1.1g
- Protein 17.9g

Fish and Tomato

GLUTEN-FREE

The tomatoes gravy adds a very sweet and tangy flavor to the recipe.
The recipe flavor is divine with great textures.

Servings: 6
Prep Time: 20 minutes
Cook Time: 12 minutes
Pressure Level: Low

Ingredient

- 1 cup water
- 1 cup tomato sauce
- 1 cup fresh tomato, chopped
- 1 teaspoon garlic
- 2 teaspoons oregano leaves
- 2 pounds of whitefish steaks, sliced
- 1 cup green bell pepper
- Salt and black pepper, to taste
- 2 cups boiled rice
- 2 onions, chopped

Directions

1. Combine all the listed ingredients in an instant pot and set timer manually for 12 minutes.
2. Afterwards, naturally releasing the steam.
3. Serve the stew over the boiled rice and enjoy.

Nutrition Facts (Per Serving)

- Calories 348
- Total Fat 9.6g
- Total Carbohydrate 30g
- Dietary Fiber 5.2g
- Protein 32.49g

Coconut Gravy with Shrimp

GLUTEN-FREE

The addition of coconut milk makes this recipe a mouth-watering experience to enjoy.

Servings: 5
Prep Time: 20 minutes
Cook Time: 7 minutes
Pressure Level: High

Ingredients

- 2 tablespoons vegetable oil
- ½ tablespoon of minced garlic
- 1 lime leaves
- 4 cups shrimps, fresh and washed
- 2 tablespoons of fish sauce
- Pinch of black pepper
- Salt, to taste
- 2 large onions
- 2 red chilies, sliced
- 2 cups of coconut milk
- 2 pieces of Galangal, 1 inch
- 1 cup of lemongrass (cut into 4-inch pieces)

Directions

1. Press the sauté button of instant pot and cook onion in oil for 1 minutes.
2. Then add in garlic, red chili, lemongrass, lime leaves, galangal, shrimp, fish sauce, salt, and pepper.
3. Let it cook for 5 minutes at high pressure.
4. Quick release the steam and add the coconut milk.
5. Stir in few times and cook it for one minute.
6. Just before serving the dish, remove lemongrass stick, lime leaves, and Galangal pieces.
7. Serve hot and enjoy.

Nutrition Facts (Per Serving)

- Calories 370
- Total Fat 29.3g
- Total Carbohydrate 17.6g
- Dietary Fiber 3.9g
- Protein 13.7g

Instant Pot Salmon

GLUTEN-FREE

It is a simple salmon recipe with the tanginess of lemon. It is a very light recipe to enjoy anytime you liked.

Servings: 4
Prep Time: 10 minutes
Cook Time: 5 minutes
Pressure Level: High

Ingredients

- 2 lemon juice
- ¾ cup of water
- 1 tablespoon of unsalted butter
- Salt and pepper to taste
- 1 cup brown rice, cooked
- 4 Salmon fillets, about 8 Oz. Each

Directions

1 Place fresh lemon juice, water in instant pot and place salmon on top of the steamer.
2 Sprinkle salt and pepper on top.
3 Lock the Instant Pot lid and set the timer for 5 minutes at high pressure.
4 Quick Release the valve to let the pressure release.
5 Serve immediately with butter and rice.
6 Enjoy.

Nutrition Facts (Per Serving)

- Calories 439
- Total Fat 15.3g
- Total Carbohydrate 36.7g
- Dietary Fiber 1.7g
- Protein 38.3g

Instant Pot Fish

GLUTEN-FREE

Steamed scallion prepared in the rich ginger, soy-sauce dressing. The hit combination of black bean paste and fish sauce takes this recipe to another level.

Servings: 5
Prep Time: 45 minutes
Cook Time: 10 minutes
Pressure Level: Low

Ingredients for sauce

- 2 tablespoons of fish sauce
- ½ teaspoon garlic
- 2 tablespoons of black bean paste, any version
- 2 tablespoons Rice wine
- ½ teaspoon ginger, minced

Vegetables Ingredients

- 2 tablespoons peanut oil
- 1 tablespoon ginger, julienned
- 1/3 cup scallions, julienned
- Handful of cilantro, chopped

- 1 pound firm white fish such as Tilapia

Directions

1 Mix all the sauce ingredients in the bowl.
2 Pour it over the fish.
3 Let it marinate for 30 minutes.
4 Next, cut all the vegetables in a separate bowl.
5 Pour 2 cups of water and adjust the steamer in the basket.
6 Place the fish inside the basket.
7 Store the marinade sauce.
8 Let the fish cook for 4 minutes at low pressure.
9 Release pressure naturally.
10 Heat oil in a pan and stir-fry vegetables.
11 Add the reserved marinade to the pan and let it cook for a few minutes.
12 Pour it over, and serve immediately.

Nutrition Facts (Per Serving)

- Calories 333
- Total Fat 30.2g
- Total Carbohydrate 4.7g
- Dietary Fiber 0.3g
- Protein 12g

Instant Pot Clams & Corn

GLUTEN-FREE

It is one of the best clams and corn recipe to enjoy.

The corns are buttered and then added t the recipe for extra creaminess and flavors.

Servings: 6
Prep Time: 20 minutes
Cook Time: 10 minutes
Pressure Level: High

Ingredients

- 1 pound clams
- 2 corns on the cob with butter
- Handful of chopped parsley
- Water, as needed
- 1 cup Dry white wine
- 1 teaspoon of garlic, minced

Directions

1   Place dry white wine, garlic, and parsley on the bottom of an instant pot.
2   Bring all the ingredients to a boil.
3   Then add one cup of water.
4   Place the steamer basket in a Pot and put clams and corn in a steam basket.
5   Cook on high pressure for 5 minutes.

6   Pour juice from the bottom of the pot onto the corn and calms.

7   Serve.

Nutrition Facts (Per Serving)

- Calories 125
- Total Fat 1.4g
- Total Carbohydrate 20.8g
- Dietary Fiber 0.6g
- Protein 2.3g

Pressure Cooker Style Divine Salmon

GLUTEN-FREE

Salmon prepared in thick and delicious gravy in just 15 minutes. It is a very light and flavorful seafood recipe to serve as dinner.

Servings: 6
Prep Time: 50 minutes
Cook Time: 15 minutes
Pressure Level: High

Ingredients

- 2 salmon fillets, 10 Oz each
- 2 cloves of garlic, minced
- 1 tablespoon ginger, grated
- 1 tablespoon brown sugar
- 1 teaspoons sesame seeds
- 1 teaspoons French Whole Grain Mustard
- 1 tablespoon of corn starch+2 tablespoons of water
- ½ cup soy sauce (*May contain a gluten!*)
- 1/3 Cup water
- ½ cup sherry
- 2 tablespoons sesame oil

Direction

1 Take a small bowl and add soy sauce, water, sherry, oil, seeds, mustard, garlic, ginger and brown sugar.
2 Mix to dissolve the sugar.
3 Place salmon in two 8 inch mini loaf pans.
4 Pour half of the prepared marinade over the salmon.
5 Marinate salmon for 30 minutes in the fridge.
6 Place trivet inside the pot and add one cup of water.
7 Place the fish along with pan on a trivet and cook on high pressure for 10 minutes.
8 Heat reserved sauce in a pan.
9 Mix cornstarch with water and add it to the pan to make the thick gravy.
10 After the 10 minutes, quick release steam.
11 Pour the cornstarch sauce over cooked fish.
12 Enjoy.

Nutrition Facts (Per Serving)

- Calories 316
- Total Fat 16.6g
- Total Carbohydrate 10.1g
- Dietary Fiber 0.8g
- Protein 30.2g

Chapter 6: Beans and Grains

Black Beans with Olives and Lemon

VEGAN   **VEGETARIAN**   **GLUTEN-FREE**

A simple salad version of the black bean is introduced in this recipe. We have kept the calories content as low as possible to make it healthy version.

Servings: 6
Prep Time: 30 minutes
Cook Time: 25 minutes
Pressure Level: High

Ingredients

- 2 cups dry black beans
- ½ teaspoon sea salt, fine
- 2 cups water
- ½ teaspoon of Chili powder
- 1 teaspoon of lemon juice
- ½ cup chopped onions
- Handful of cilantro
- ½ cup halved green olives

Directions

1 Combine salt, water, and beans in the Instant Pot and stir to combine.
2 Manually set the Instant Pot to 25 minutes at high pressure.
3 Quickly release the steam.
4 Drain the beans and add lemon juice, chili powder, onion, olives, and cilantro.
5 Serve and enjoy.

Nutrition Facts (Per Serving)

- Calories 227
- Total Fat 1g
- Total Carbohydrate 41.7g
- Dietary Fiber 10.3g
- Protein 14.3g

Refried Beans

VEGAN   **VEGETARIAN**   **GLUTEN-FREE**

Pinto beans are prepared in some finest herbs and spices, which give a perfect aroma to this simple dish.

Servings: 6
Prep Time: 50 minutes
Cook Time: 30 minutes
Pressure Level: High

Ingredients

- 2 cups pinto beans, sorted and rinsed
- 2 medium onions
- 4 cups filtered water
- 2 cloves garlic, chopped
- ½ cup avocado oil
- Black pepper, to taste
- 2 jalapeños, minced
- ½ tablespoon sea salt

Directions

1. Turn the Instant Pot to Sauté mode.
2. Sauté the onion, garlic, and jalapeño in the avocado oil, then add the water, sea salt, pepper, and beans.
3. Cook on high pressure for 30 minutes.
4. Use a quick release method to release the pressure.
5. Open the pot and mash and stir the beans.
6. Cook down for a few minutes until your refried beans are thickened.
7. Serve and enjoy.

Nutrition Facts (Per Serving)

- Calories 267
- Total Fat 3.2g
- Total Carbohydrate 45.7g
- Dietary Fiber 11.8g
- Protein 14.6g

No-Soak Simple Beans

VEGAN   VEGETARIAN   GLUTEN-FREE

It is a very tasty recipe to enjoy. You can serve it with boiled rice or enjoy it as it is.

Servings: 4
Prep Time: 50 minutes
Cook Time: 40 minutes
Pressure Level: High

Ingredients

- 1-pound beans, dried
- 2 cups water
- 2 tablespoons olive oil
- ½ teaspoon salt
- 1 teaspoon of garlic, optional
- 1 tsp bay leaf, optional

Directions

1. Add all the listed ingredients in the pot.
2. Cook on high pressure for 40 minutes.
3. Once beep sounds, quick release the steam.
4. Open the pot and slightly mash the beans.
5. Serve into bowls and enjoy.

Nutrition Facts (Per Serving)

- Calories 98
- Total Fat 7.2g
- Total Carbohydrate 8.7g
- Dietary Fiber 4g
- Protein 2.2g

Simple Bean Soup

GLUTEN-FREE

It is very low fat and high protein recipe to enjoy. It is no doubt a recipe rich in protein, fats, carbohydrates, and minerals.

Servings: 2
Prep Time: 30 minutes
Cook Time: 22 minutes
Pressure Level: High

Ingredients

- 1.5 cups bean soup mix
- 1 ham bone
- 1 onion, chopped
- 1 large diced tomato
- 1 cup carrots, diced
- 1/3 cup celery, diced
- 1 teaspoon chili powder
- 2 teaspoons garlic powder
- ½ teaspoon sea salt
- 1/3 teaspoon pepper
- 3 cups water

Directions

1. Place beans soup mix in a pot and add 3 cups of water and cook at high pressure for 12 minutes.
2. Now open the pot and add the ham bone.
3. Cover the pot and cook on the bean setting with a natural release method.
4. Afterward, remove the ham bone and add all the remaining listed ingredients.
5. Cook for 10 minutes at high pressure.
6. Then serve and enjoy.

Nutrition Facts (Per Serving)

- Calories 255
- Total Fat 6.4g
- Total Carbohydrate 37.1g
- Dietary Fiber 7.7g
- Protein 13.4g

Instant Pot White Beans Mix

VEGAN   VEGETARIAN   GLUTEN-FREE

It is a simple recipe that can enjoy a perfectly with boiled rice. You can have it as lunch or even as dinner.

Servings: 6
Prep Time: 15 minutes
Cook Time: 45 minutes
Pressure Level: High

Ingredients

- ½ pound white beans
- ½ small onion, minced
- 2-4 cloves garlic, minced
- 1/3 cup molasses
- 1/3 cup maple syrup
- 2 tablespoons mustard powder
- 1/6 cup balsamic vinegar
- 1/3 teaspoon ground pepper
- 4 cups of water or more
- Sea salt, to taste

Directions

1. Place beans and water in the pot and cook it on high pressure for 10 minutes.
2. Drain and rinse the beans, then place them back into the Instant Pot.

3   Cover the beans with a generous amount of water and add the remaining listed ingredients.

4   Cook for 45 minutes.

5   Then release the steam naturally.

6   Serve and enjoy.

Nutrition Facts (Per Serving)

- Calories 249
- Total Fat 1.5g
- Total Carbohydrate 50.8g
- Dietary Fiber 6.5g
- Protein 10g

Black Beans Recipe

VEGAN   **VEGETARIAN**   **GLUTEN-FREE**

It is a vegan recipe that includes some best whole food items. The hit combination of herbs and spices makes this recipe a classic hit.

Servings: 4
Prep Time: 20 minutes
Cook Time: 20 minutes
Pressure Level: High

Ingredients

- 1 pound of Black Beans, sorted and rinsed
- 2 tablespoons onion powder
- 1 teaspoon garlic powder
- ¼ teaspoons salt
- 2 bay leaves
- 6 cups vegetable broth or chicken broth

Directions

1. Add all the listed ingredients in your Instant Pot.
2. Lock the lid of the pot and then turn the valve to seal.
3. Press the "Beans" button.
4. When the time complete, quick release the steam.
5. Next, turn the valve to venting.
6. Enjoy beans over cooked rice.

Nutrition Facts (Per Serving)

- Calories 196
- Total Fat 1.7g
- Total Carbohydrate 34.7g
- Dietary Fiber 11.8g
- Protein 12g

Black Bean Soup Recipe

VEGAN   **VEGETARIAN**   **GLUTEN-FREE**

It is a simple and easy soup recipe to enjoy. The best soup to enjoy that is prepared with some finest ingredients.

Servings: 6
Prep Time: 50 minutes
Cook Time: 40 minutes
Pressure Level: High

Ingredients

- 2 teaspoons butter, or coconut oil
- ½ onion, finely chopped
- 2 garlic cloves, minced
- 4 celery ribs, chopped
- 2-4 carrots, chopped
- 1/2 large red bell pepper, chopped
- 4-6 cups water or more to thin
- 2 cups black beans, (soaked for 2 hours)
- ½ teaspoon sea salt, plus more to taste
- 1 teaspoon cumin
- 1 lemon, juiced

Directions

1. Take a large instant pot and heat it over medium heat.
2. Then add all the listed ingredients into the pot and cook at high pressure for 35-40 minutes.
3. Next release the steam naturally.
4. Puree about a cup of the cooked mixture with the help of a blender, and add it to the remaining mixture in the instant pot.
5. Serve hot and enjoy.

Nutrition Facts (Per Serving)

- Calories 265
- Total Fat 2.6g
- Total Carbohydrate 47.7g
- Dietary Fiber 11.6g
- Protein 14.8g

Gingerbread Squares

VEGAN   VEGETARIAN   GLUTEN-FREE

Very highly nutrition bar to enjoy and they are a good alternative to processed or artificial energy bars.

Servings: 6
Prep Time: 60 minutes
Cook Time: 45 minutes
Pressure Level: High

Ingredients

- 2 cups black beans
- 1 cup oat flour, gluten-free
- 1/3 cup coconut oil, melted
- 2/4 cup coconut sugar
- ½ teaspoon ginger, ground
- 1 teaspoon cinnamon, ground
- 1/4 teaspoon cloves, ground
- 1/4 teaspoon salt
- 1/4 teaspoon baking soda
- ½ teaspoon vanilla extract
- ½ tablespoon blackstrap molasses
- 2-4 teaspoons apple cider vinegar
- 1 tablespoon of brown sugar

Directions

1. Soak the beans for the few hours in a generous amount of water.
2. Add beans into the instant pot and cook on high pressure for 30 minutes.
3. Open the pot and drain the beans.
4. In a bowl, add the entire remaining listed ingredient along with beans.
5. Pulse it for 3 minutes in a blender.
6. Now flatten the mixture into a flat baking dish lined with parchment paper.
7. Complete in the oven by baking at 350°F for 15 minutes.
8. Remove the dish from the oven and then slice as desired.
9. Serve and enjoy.

Nutrition Facts (Per Serving)

- Calories 439
- Total Fat 14.1g
- Total Carbohydrate 64.8g
- Dietary Fiber 11.6g
- Protein 16g

Chapter 7: Fast and Easy Snacks and Appetizers

Garlic, pepper, and Almonds

VEGAN   **VEGETARIAN**   **GLUTEN-FREE**

It is a very healthy nut snack to enjoy. Once you try it surely, you will ask for more.

Servings: 6

Prep Time: 20 minutes

Cook Time: 15 minutes

Pressure Level: High

Ingredients

- 6 cups almonds, whole
- 2 tablespoons butter, melted (or vegetable oil)
- 4 cloves garlic, minced
- 2 teaspoons pepper, coarse ground

Directions

1. Heat butter in an instant pot by turning it on.
2. Then add almonds, garlic, and pepper.
3. Stir and combine.
4. Cover the pot and cook on low heat for 15 minutes.
5. Natural release the steam.
6. Once done serve and enjoy.

Nutrition Facts (Per Serving)

- Calories 588
- Total Fat 51.4g
- Total Carbohydrate 21.5g
- Dietary Fiber 12.1g
- Protein 20.3g

Glazed Nuts

VEGAN   **VEGETARIAN**   **GLUTEN-FREE**

The sweet and salty combination is introduced in this recipe. It is a satisfying meal to enjoy.

Servings: 5
Prep Time: 10 minutes
Cook Time: 10 minutes
Pressure Level: High

Ingredients

- 2 tablespoons butter, melted (or vegetable oil)
- 1/3 cup brown sugar
- ½ teaspoon cinnamon, grounded
- 2 teaspoons five-spice, powder
- 1/4 teaspoon salt
- 20 pieces pecans, halves

Directions

1. Mix butter, sugar, cinnamon, spice and pecans in a bowl.
2. Mix to combine all ingredients well.
3. Cover and cook on high 10 minutes.
4. Open and serve.
5. Enjoy.

Nutrition Facts (Per Serving)

- Calories 550
- Total Fat 53.8g
- Total Carbohydrate 17.7g
- Dietary Fiber 6.1g
- Protein 6.2g

Potato in Instant Pot

VEGAN   VEGETARIAN   GLUTEN-FREE

It is a very healthy version of potatoes to enjoy. You can serve it with your favorite dipping sauce.

Servings: 5
Prep Time: 50 minutes
Cook Time: 10 minutes
Pressure Level: High

Ingredient

- 5 pounds Potatoes, peeled
- 1 cup water
- shallot

Direction

1. Place the steamer basket in instant pot.
2. Add in water and place potatoes in the steamer basket.
3. Close the lid.
4. Turn the vent to seal.
5. Set timer for 10 minutes at high pressure.
6. Open the pot by quick release steam.
7. Open the lid, sprinkle with shallot and eat the potatoes with your favorite sauce.

Nutrition Facts (Per Serving)

- Calories 313
- Total Fat 0.5g
- Total Carbohydrate 71.3g
- Dietary Fiber 10.9g
- Protein 7.6g

Curried Party Mix

VEGETARIAN   GLUTEN-FREE

The true flavor of curry can be experienced in this snack recipe. Do not hesitate to make it right away.

Servings: 6
Prep Time: 5 minutes
Cook Time: 2 minutes
Pressure Level: High

Ingredients

- 2 cups rice cereal squares
- ½ cup sesame sticks
- 1 cup cashews
- 1 cup honey
- 1 cup roasted peanuts
- 2 tablespoons butter, melted
- 1 teaspoon of soy sauce *(May contain a gluten!)*
- 1 teaspoon of curry powder
- 1 teaspoon of brown sugar

Directions

1. Turn on the sauté mode of instant pot and add the entire listed ingredient in it.
2. Cook on high for 2 minutes.

3. Quickly release the steam.

4. Line a parchment paper on to a flat dish.

5. Transfer the instant pot mixture to the dish and press it with a spatula to make it even.

6. Let it cool so it gets hard, and then cut into square shapes.

7. Serve and enjoy.

Nutrition Facts (Per Serving)

- Calories 614
- Total Fat 33.4g
- Total Carbohydrate 75.2g
- Dietary Fiber 3.5g
- Protein 12.8g

Simple Bacon Egg Cups

GLUTEN-FREE

Egg and bacon are combined to prepare this fine recipe that can be enjoyed as an appetizer.

Servings: 8
Prep Time: 30 minutes
Cook Time: 7 minutes
Pressure Level: High

Ingredients

- 8 organic eggs
- 8 slices bacon
- 4 Oz. Cheese
- Salt and fresh black pepper, to taste

Directions

1. Place a steamer basket in the instant pot.
2. Add in the water.
3. Place bacon strips in the muffin silicon cups.
4. Crack one egg into each hole and sprinkle cheese, salt, and black pepper.
5. Place the muffin cup in a steamer basket.
6. Cover the pot and set the timer for 7 minutes at high pressure.
7. Open the pot and quick release the steam.
8. Remove muffins from steamer basket and serve hot.

Nutrition Facts (Per Serving)

- Calories 262
- Total Fat 22.6g
- Total Carbohydrate 0.9g
- Dietary Fiber 0g
- Protein 13.4g

Instant Pot Kale Salad

VEGETARIAN   GLUTEN-FREE

It is a very easy to make kale salad recipe, which can be enjoyed as a snack or appetizer. The recipe is cheesy, creamy, lemony and healthy. Sure, your taste buds will have a roller coaster ride of flavors.

Servings: 4
Prep Time: 35 minutes
Cook Time: 25 minutes
Pressure Level: High to low

Ingredients

- 1 tablespoon olive oil
- 1.3-pound kale, cleaned and stems trimmed
- Salt, to taste
- 2 cups potatoes, cubed
- 1 cup cheddar cheese, cubed
- Juice squeezed from 1/2 a lemon
- Fresh ground black pepper

Directions

1. Wash the vegetables well before starting the cooking process.
2. Place the trivet inside the instant pot and add two cups of water.
3. Place potatoes on top of the trivet.

4. Close the instant pot lid, and let it cook for 20 minutes at high pressure.
5. Open the pot by quickly releasing the steam.
6. Take out the potatoes from the trivet.
7. Cut the kale in to bite size pieces and place it on top of trivet
8. Close the instant pot and set manual to 3 minutes at low pressure.
9. Afterward, open the pot and add kale to the steamed potatoes.
10. Arrange the vegetables in a bowl and sprinkle salt and pepper.
11. Drizzle oil and lemon juice on top and then add in the cheddar cheese cubes.
12. Mix well and serve.

Nutrition Facts (Per Serving)

- Calories 271
- Total Fat 13g
- Total Carbohydrate 27.8g
- Dietary Fiber 4.1g
- Protein 12.8g

Cajun Mixed Nuts

VEGETARIAN   GLUTEN-FREE

Here we have introduced a very simple and delicious sweet and spicy mixed nut to enjoy. It is a recipe rich in multivitamins, fiber, calcium, protein, and potassium.

Servings: 4
Prep Time: 25 minutes
Cook Time: 15 minutes
Pressure Level: low

Main Ingredients

- 2 cups pecans halves and raw
- 2 tablespoons butter
- 1 tablespoon Water
- 1 cup almonds, raw
- 1 cup peanuts, raw
- ½ cup maple syrup
- 1 tablespoon spicy Cajun seasoning
- Sea salt, to taste
- ½ cup of raw cashews

Other ingredients

- 10 ounces dried mango, slices

Directions

1. Combine all the main ingredients in an instant pot (except water), and turn on its sauté mode.
2. Once the butter melts, pour in the water.
3. Close the pot and set the timer to 10 minutes at low pressure.
4. Open the pot and transfer the mixture to an oil greased baking tray.
5. Bake in the oven at 390°F for 5 minutes.
6. Once the nuts turn brown, take it out from the oven and add in the dried mango slices.
7. Enjoy.

Nutrition Facts (Per Serving)

- Calories 318
- Total Fat 27g
- Total Carbohydrate 14.6g
- Dietary Fiber 4g
- Protein 9.4g

Snack Time Pear

VEGAN　　　**VEGETARIAN**　　　**GLUTEN-FREE**

It is a simple recipe that can be enjoyed at snack time. The pear tastes divine, as it collects all the liquids and juices during the cooking process.

Servings: 4

Prep Time: 5 minutes

Cook Time: 7 minutes

Pressure Level: High

Ingredient

- 4 large pears
- ½ cup raisins
- 1 cup red wine
- 6 tablespoons brown sugar
- 1/3 teaspoon ground cinnamon

Directions

1. Place the pears in the bottom of the instant pot.
2. Next pour in wine, sugar, cinnamon, and raisins into the pot.
3. Cook at high pressure for 7 minutes.
4. Quick release steam and then serve it with a lot of cooking liquid from the bottom of the pot.
5. Enjoy.

Nutrition Facts (Per Serving)

- Calories 251
- Total Fat 0.3g
- Total Carbohydrate 54g
- Dietary Fiber 5.9g
- Protein 1.2g

Eggplant with Yogurt

VEGETARIAN   GLUTEN-FREE

It is a very light and refreshing appetizer recipe bursting with multivitamins. The taste is great, and the texture is creamy and delicious.

Servings: 3

Prep Time: 10 minutes

Cook Time: 2 minutes

Pressure Level: High

Ingredients

- 2 large eggplants, peeled
- ½ cup red tomato, finely chopped
- 4 tablespoons olive oil
- 2 tablespoons lemon juice
- Salt and pepper, to taste
- 1 cup onion, chopped
- 2 cups Greek yogurt
- 2 cloves of garlic, minced

Directions

1. Place the trivet inside the instant pot and add two cups of water.
2. Place the eggplants on to the trivet, and cook for 2 minutes at high pressure.
3. Next, quick release the steam.
4. Take out the eggplants and then mash it with the help of a fork.

5. Place it in a bowl and add the remaining listed ingredient to it.

6. Mix well, and serve this refreshing appetizer recipe.

Nutrition Facts (Per Serving)

- Calories 867
- Total Fat 35 g
- Total Carbohydrate 55.8g
- Dietary Fiber 12.1g
- Protein 85 g

Popcorns

VEGAN   VEGETARIAN   GLUTEN-FREE

Popcorns are full of healthy nutrients and a very light snack to enjoy. It is one of the most favorite snacks to enjoy by many.

Servings: 4

Prep Time: 30 minutes

Cook Time: 10 minutes

Pressure Level: High

Ingredients

- 1 cup popcorn kernels, unpopped
- 2 teaspoons of coconut oil
- 1 tablespoon of butter (*use 1 teaspoon coconut oil for vegans*)

Directions

1. Turn on the sauté button and then push adjusts to more.
2. When the display reads hot, add the butter and coconut oil.
3. Stir for one minute.
4. Add popcorn kernels and stir to combine.
5. Put the lid on the pot.
6. When the popping is slowed down, turn off the pot.
7. Before removing the lid finish popping.
8. Enjoy.

Nutrition Facts (Per Serving)

- Calories 196
- Total Fat 7.1g
- Total Carbohydrate 30.82g
- Dietary Fiber 3g
- Protein 3.94g

Chapter 8: Desserts

<u>Simple and Classic Carrot Cake</u>

VEGETARIAN   **GLUTEN-FREE**

Here we have introduced a best and most easy carrot cake recipe that just takes 10 minutes to cook.

Servings: 8
Prep Time: 20 minutes
Cook Time: 10 minutes
Pressure Level: High

Ingredients

- 2 cups almond meal
- 1/3 cup plain flour
- Pinch of salt
- 2-4 tablespoons of butter
- 1 cup maple syrup
- 1 egg, whisked
- 1 cup coconut milk
- ½ teaspoon baking soda
- 1 cup carrots, grated

Directions

1. Add a steamer basket to the instant pot.
2. Add 2 cups of water to the pot.
3. Grease a cake pan with oil spray.
4. In a bowl, combine meal, flours, salt, and soda in a bowl.
5. Combine all the other ingredients in the other bowl.
6. Place it inside the pot into the steamer basket.
7. Select the high pressure for 10 minutes.
8. Afterwards, turn it off.
9. Quick pressure releases.
10. Remove carrot cake from steamer basket.
11. Serve and enjoy.

Nutrition Facts (Per Serving)

- Calories 385
- Total Fat 21.6g
- Total Carbohydrate 38.34g
- Dietary Fiber 4.4g
- Protein 6.78g

Easy Brownies

VEGETARIAN   **GLUTEN-FREE**

It is a very simple recipe that needs no baking. It's a treat for all chocolate lovers.

Servings: 6

Prep Time: 30 minutes

Cook Time: 12 minutes

Pressure Level: High

Ingredients

- 22 Oz. Brownie mix (*May contain gluten, please read ingredients*)
- 2 tablespoons butter, melted
- ½ cup chopped walnuts

Directions

1. Combine all the listed ingredients in a bowl.
2. Grease a 7-inch pan with butter.
3. Pour mix mixture into pan.
4. Place it on the rack in the pot.
5. Cover and cook on high for 12 minutes.
6. Then use a quick pressure release.
7. Open the lid of the pot.
8. Remove the cake and serve.

Nutrition Facts (Per Serving)

- Calories 549
- Total Fat 25.5g
- Total Carbohydrate 80.7g
- Dietary Fiber 0.7g
- Protein 6.7g

Lemony Bites

VEGETARIAN

It is a simple lemony bite to prepare in just 12 minutes. You will surely enjoy making and eat one.

Servings: 6
Prep Time: 20 minutes
Cook Time: 12 minutes
Pressure Level: High

Ingredients

- 9 Oz. Yellow cake mix
- 1 egg
- 1 tablespoon butter
- 4 ounces cream cheese
- 4 tablespoons stevia
- ½ teaspoon vanilla
- 1 tablespoon lemon zest
- 1/4 teaspoon salt

Directions

1. Beat cream cheese, stevia, and vanilla in a bowl until smooth.
2. Then add flour, zest, egg, butter, and salt.
3. Pour it into the oil greased pan.

4. Place pan on rack in 6-quart instant pot.

5. Cover and cook on high for 12 minutes.

6. Cut into squares.

7. Serve and enjoy.

Nutrition Facts (Per Serving)

- Calories 418
- Total Fat 21.3g
- Total Carbohydrate 51g
- Dietary Fiber 0.8g
- Protein 6.4g

Strawberry and Rhubarb Compote

VEGAN   **VEGETARIAN**   **GLUTEN-FREE**

The combination of strawberries with rhubarb makes it unique and mouthwatering experience to enjoy.

Servings: 6

Prep Time: 5 minutes

Cook Time: 15 minutes

Pressure Level: High

Ingredients

- 1.3 pounds strawberries
- 1.5 pounds rhubarb
- 1/3 cup stevia
- 1/3 cup of water

Directions

1. Combine all ingredients in the instant pot.
2. Cook on high pressure for 10 minutes.
3. Once a thick consistency is obtained sauté it for 5 minutes.
4. Serve and enjoy.

Nutrition Facts (Per Serving)

- Calories 55
- Total Fat 0.5g
- Total Carbohydrate 12.7g
- Dietary Fiber 4g
- Protein 1.7g

Baked Apples

VEGETARIAN   **GLUTEN-FREE**

It is a simple yet delicious recipe to enjoy. You can use brown sugar instead of stevia.

Servings: 6
Prep Time: 10 minutes
Cook Time: 6 minutes
Pressure Level: High

Ingredient

- 6 large baking apples
- 1 cup dried fruit
- 2 pecans
- 4 teaspoons stevia
- 2 tablespoons honey
- 1/3 teaspoon ground cinnamon
- 1/5 teaspoon ground nutmeg
- 6 tablespoons butter

Directions

1. Wash and center core the apples.
2. Place dry fruits, toasted Pecans, stevia, cinnamon, nutmeg and butter in the pot.
3. Fill apples with this mixture.
4. Place it in an instant pot.
5. Cook on high for 6 minutes.
6. Serve and enjoy.

Nutrition Facts (Per Serving)

- Calories 310
- Total Fat 15.3g
- Total Carbohydrate 46.8g
- Dietary Fiber 7.8g
- Protein 2.1g

Chocolate Fondue

VEGETARIAN   **GLUTEN-FREE**

If you love fondues, then try this recipe by using instant pot as it makes the cooking process efficient.

Servings: 6

Prep Time: 10 minutes

Cook Time: 7 minutes

Pressure Level: High

Ingredients

- 32 Oz. Dark chocolate
- 1 cup light cream
- 4 tablespoons rum
- Dippers: whole strawberries, fruit pieces

Directions

1. Place chocolate and light cream in your instant pot.
2. Cook at high for 7 minutes.
3. Quick release steam.
4. Then add the rum.
5. Serve with fruit pieces.

Nutrition Facts (Per Serving)

- Calories 897
- Total Fat 51.1g
- Total Carbohydrate 92.4g
- Dietary Fiber 5.7g
- Protein 12.2g

Fruit Compote

VEGAN   VEGETARIAN   GLUTEN-FREE

It is a recipe that gives your taste bud a roller coaster ride of flavors. It is a
very fruity recipe to make.

Servings: 2

Prep Time: 10 minutes

Cook Time: 7 minutes

Pressure Level: High

Ingredients

- 8 Oz. Dried fruit
- 2 Pears
- ½ lemon, thinly sliced
- 2 cups apple juice
- 1 tsp cinnamon
- 1 tsp whole cloves
- 1/8 teaspoon salt

Directions

1. Combine all the listed ingredients in your instant pot.
2. Cook on high for 7 minutes.
3. Serve warm or room temperature. □

Nutrition Facts (Per Serving)

- Calories 454
- Total Fat 0.9g
- Total Carbohydrate 116.8g
- Dietary Fiber 14.4g
- Protein 4.2g

Caramel Fondue

VEGETARIAN   **GLUTEN-FREE**

It is a simple recipe with some classic taste. Enjoy it with your favorites dipping items.

Servings: 6

Prep Time: 10 minutes

Cook Time: 8 minutes

Pressure Level: High

Ingredients

- 4 cups caramel ice cream topping
- 1 jar marshmallow cream
- 1 cup raisins
- 4 tablespoons light rum

Directions

1. Combine all the listed ingredients in your instant pot.
2. Cook at high pressure for 8 minutes.
3. Serve warm.

Nutrition Facts (Per Serving)

- Calories 676
- Total Fat 0.32g
- Total Carbohydrate 169.56g
- Dietary Fiber 2g
- Protein 3.5g

Perfect Jam in Instant Pot

VEGAN   VEGETARIAN   GLUTEN-FREE

A very easy and delicious jam that is prepared in instant pot and served with breadsticks.

Servings: 4
Prep Time: 5 minutes
Cook Time: 4 minutes
Pressure Level: High

Ingredients

- 1.5 pounds blueberries, fresh or frozen
- 6 scoops stevia
- Water, as needed

Directions

1. Add blueberries and stevia in an instant pot along with a few teaspoons of water.
2. Turn on the sauté function of the pot.
3. When it boils, place the lid on top.
4. Set timer for 2 minutes at high pressure.
5. Once timer beeps, use a natural release to release the steam.
6. Pour jam into clean glass jars.
7. Serve as a snack with little bread sticks.

Nutrition Facts (Per Serving)

- Calories 32
- Total Fat 0.2g
- Total Carbohydrate 8.2g
- Dietary Fiber 1.4g
- Protein 0.4g

Chapter 9: Yogurt Recipes

Simple and Plain Yogurt

VEGETARIAN   **GLUTEN-FREE**

It is a very simple yet mouth-watering yogurt that is made with just two ingredients.

Servings: 6
Prep Time: 50 minutes
Cook Time: 9 hours
Pressure Level: High

Ingredients

- 16 cups of whole plain cow's milk
- 4 tablespoons yogurt, plain

Directions

1. Take an instant pot and add milk to it.
2. Cover the pot and press the yogurt setting.
3. Set it to boil.
4. When the timer beeps or the boiling stage, let it sit for 5 -10 minutes.
5. Turn off your instant pot.
6. Open the pot and remove its steel bowl.
7. Let it stand at room temperature until temperature reaches 110° F.
8. Keep stirring the bowl when it's set at room temperature.
9. Take a bowl and add yogurt to it.
10. Add yogurt to a large bowl and stir in the warm milk about 2/3 cup.
11. Pour this mixture to remaining milk.
12. Place it in a pot and cover it tightly.
13. Then turn the "Yogurt" setting.
14. When the timer off turns the pot off.
15. Remove the lid of the instant pot.
16. Transfer the yogurt to a bowl and let it chill for 9 hours before serving.

Nutrition Facts (Per Serving)

- Calories 333
- Total Fat 13.5g
- Total Carbohydrate 32.7g
- Dietary Fiber 0g
- Protein 21.9g

Coconut Milk Yogurt

VEGETARIAN   **GLUTEN-FREE**

The coconut milk is a part of the recipe that makes it a very nutritious yogurt to try. You can serve it with shredded coconut flakes if liked.

Servings: 2
Prep Time: 50 minutes
Cook Time: 9 hours
Pressure Level: High

Ingredients

- 2 cups of coconut cream, Un-sweetened
- 1 package of yogurt starter
- 1 tablespoon of gelatin

Directions

1. Take an instant pot and add cream to it.
2. Cover the pot and press the yogurt setting.
3. Set it to boil.
4. When the timer beeps or the boiling stage, let it sit for 5 -10 minutes.
5. Turn off your instant pot.
6. Open the pot and remove its liner.
7. Let it stand at room temperature until temperature reache100° F.
8. Next, add in the started a little at a time.
9. Whisk it well, so no lumps form.
10. Place liner in a pot and cover it tightly.
11. Then turn the "Yogurt" setting and set to 8 hours.
12. Afterwards, add in gelatin slowly.
13. Keep stirring as you do not want the lumps to form.
14. When the timer off turns the pot off.
15. Remove the yogurt from the instant pot.
16. Transfer the yogurt to the bowl and let it chill for 9 hours before serving.

Nutrition Facts (Per Serving)

- Calories 566
- Total Fat 57.2g
- Total Carbohydrate 13.8g
- Dietary Fiber 5.3g
- Protein 8.5g

Almond Milk Yogurt

VEGAN   VEGETARIAN   GLUTEN-FREE

The addition of almond milk makes it a really healthy version of yogurt to enjoy. It is a very nutritious yogurt with certain pro-biotic good for health.

Servings: 4
Prep Time: 40 minutes
Cook Time: 9 hours
Pressure Level: High

Ingredients

- 3-4 Cups Almond Milk
- ½ Cup Raw Cashews
- 1 Tablespoon Arrowroot Powder
- 1/3 teaspoon Agar Powder
- 1/3 Cup Plain Almond yogurt

Directions

1. Blend almond milk, cashews, arrowroot powder, and agar powder in the blender and pulse for few minutes.
2. Now simmer this minute in the skillet over medium heat.
3. Transfer this mixture to a large bowl.
4. Cool to 100° F.
5. Stir in the yogurt into the bowl.
6. Wash the mason jars or another glass jar and set aside.

7. Add 2 cups of water to the instant pot and place the steamer rack inside the pot.

8. Fill the Mason jar with the prepared mixture and add to the pot.

9. Turn on the pot by pressing the yogurt.

10. Set timer to 8 hours.

11. Afterwards, refrigerate or use the yogurt once cool down.

Nutrition Facts (Per Serving)

- Calories 671
- Total Fat 65.5g
- Total Carbohydrate 22.4g
- Dietary Fiber 6.4g
- Protein 8.7g

Soy-Milk Yogurt

VEGETARIAN   GLUTEN-FREE

Here we have introduced a very easy and versatile recipe for yogurt prepared from soy milk. The recipe is rich in prebiotic sugars, that help boosts the immune system.

Servings: 4
Prep Time: 50 minutes
Cook Time: 9 hours
Pressure Level: High

Ingredients

- 5 Cups Soy Milk
- ½ Cup Cashews
- 3 Tablespoons Arrowroot Powder
- 1/3 teaspoon Agar Powder
- 1 cup maple syrup
- 1/4 Cup Coconut yogurt

Directions

1. Blend soy milk, cashews, arrowroot powder, and agar powder in the blender and pulse for few minutes.
2. Now simmer this minute in the skillet over medium heat.
3. Transfer this mixture to a large bowl.

4. Then add maple syrup and stir.

5. Cool to 100° F.

6. Stir in the yogurt into the bowl.

7. Wash the mason jars or another glass jar and set aside.

8. Add 2 cups of water to the instant pot and place the steamer rack inside the pot.

9. Fill the Mason jar with the prepared mixture and add to the pot.

10. Turn on the pot by pressing the yogurt.

11. Set timer to 8 hours.

12. Afterward, refrigerate or use the yogurt once cool down.

Nutrition Facts (Per Serving)

- Calories 506
- Total Fat 13.8g
- Total Carbohydrate 85.3g
- Dietary Fiber 2.4g
- Protein 12.9g

Maples Syrup Yogurt

VEGETARIAN   **GLUTEN-FREE**

If you like sweet yogurt, then try this recipe. It surely satisfies your cravings.

Servings: 6
Prep Time: 50 minutes
Cook Time: 9 hours
Pressure Level: High

Ingredients

- 16 cups of whole plain cow's milk
- 4 tablespoons yogurt, plain
- 1 cup maple syrup

Directions

1. Take an instant pot and add milk to it.
2. Cover the pot and press the yogurt setting.
3. Set it to boil.
4. When the timer beeps or the boiling stage, let it sit for 5 -10 minutes.
5. Turn off your instant pot.
6. Open the pot and remove its steel bowl.
7. Let it stand at room temperature until temperature reaches 110° F.
8. Add in the maple syrup.
9. Keep stirring the bowl when it's set at room temperature.
10. Take a bowl and add yogurt to it.
11. Add yogurt to a large bowl and stir in the warm milk about 2/3 cup.
12. Pour this mixture to remaining milk.
13. Place it in a pot and cover it tightly.
14. Then turn the "Yogurt" setting.
15. When the timer off turns the pot off.
16. Remove the lid of an instant pot.
17. Transfer the yogurt to the bowl and let it chill for 9 hours before serving.

Nutrition Facts (Per Serving)

- Calories 470
- Total Fat 13.6g
- Total Carbohydrate 67.9g
- Dietary Fiber 0g
- Protein 21.9g

Vanilla Yogurt

VEGETARIAN   GLUTEN-FREE

It is a very simple and delicious recipe to make in an instant pot.

Vanilla extract gives it aromatic and delicious flavor.

Servings: 6
Prep Time: 50 minutes
Cook Time: 9 hours
Pressure Level: High

Ingredients

- 2 tablespoons vanilla extract
- 16 cups of whole milk
- 4 tablespoons yogurt, plain

Directions

1. Take an instant pot and add milk to it.
2. Cover the pot and press the yogurt setting.
3. Set it to boil.
4. When the timer beeps or the boiling stage, let it sit for 5 -10 minutes.
5. Turn off your instant pot.
6. Open the pot and remove its steel bowl.
7. Let it stand at room temperature until temperature reache110° F.
8. Add in the vanilla extract.
9. Keep stirring the bowl when it's set at room temperature.

10. Take a bowl and add yogurt to it.

11. Add yogurt to a large bowl and stir in the warm milk about 2/3 cup.

12. Pour this mixture to remaining milk.

13. Place it in a pot and cover it tightly.

14. Then turn the "Yogurt" setting.

15. When the timer off turns the pot off.

16. Remove the lid of the instant pot.

17. Transfer the yogurt to a bowl and let it chill for 9 hours before serving.

Nutrition Facts (Per Serving)

- Calories 410
- Total Fat 21.3g
- Total Carbohydrate 30.7g
- Dietary Fiber 0g
- Protein 21.5g

Conclusion

I want say thanks and congratulations from the bottom of my heart for purchasing this book, which contains over 70 of the best recipes for the whole family. They will get you on your way to becoming an Instant Pot expert.

You'll be making delicious, healthy, and easy Instant Pot dishes in no time. This comprehensive book provides you with all the information necessary to kick-start your Instant Pot journey. The recipes are sorted into categories to make your daily meal planning as easy as possible.

Along with that, snippets of nutritional information are provided with each recipe so that can keep your calorie consumption on track. All that said, this book will give you all the necessary information to use the Instant Pot in the right away.

In gratitude for your purchase of this book, I want to send you a valuable & useful GIFT!

GET YOUR GIFT

EAT RIGHT! BURN FAT!

http://hudson.topbook.top/

Do you know Apple Cider Vinegar is like magic?

Whether you want to lose some weight, fight against cancer, use it as a detox or relieve the symptoms of dozens of medical conditions, using apple cider vinegar is something you should try. And with lots of recipes included, you can also get your family taking this amazing supplement without them even knowing about it.

Read **EAT RIGHT! BURN FAT! Miracle Benefits of Apple Cider Vinegar** now and see how it can help you!

Made in the USA
Middletown, DE
12 April 2018